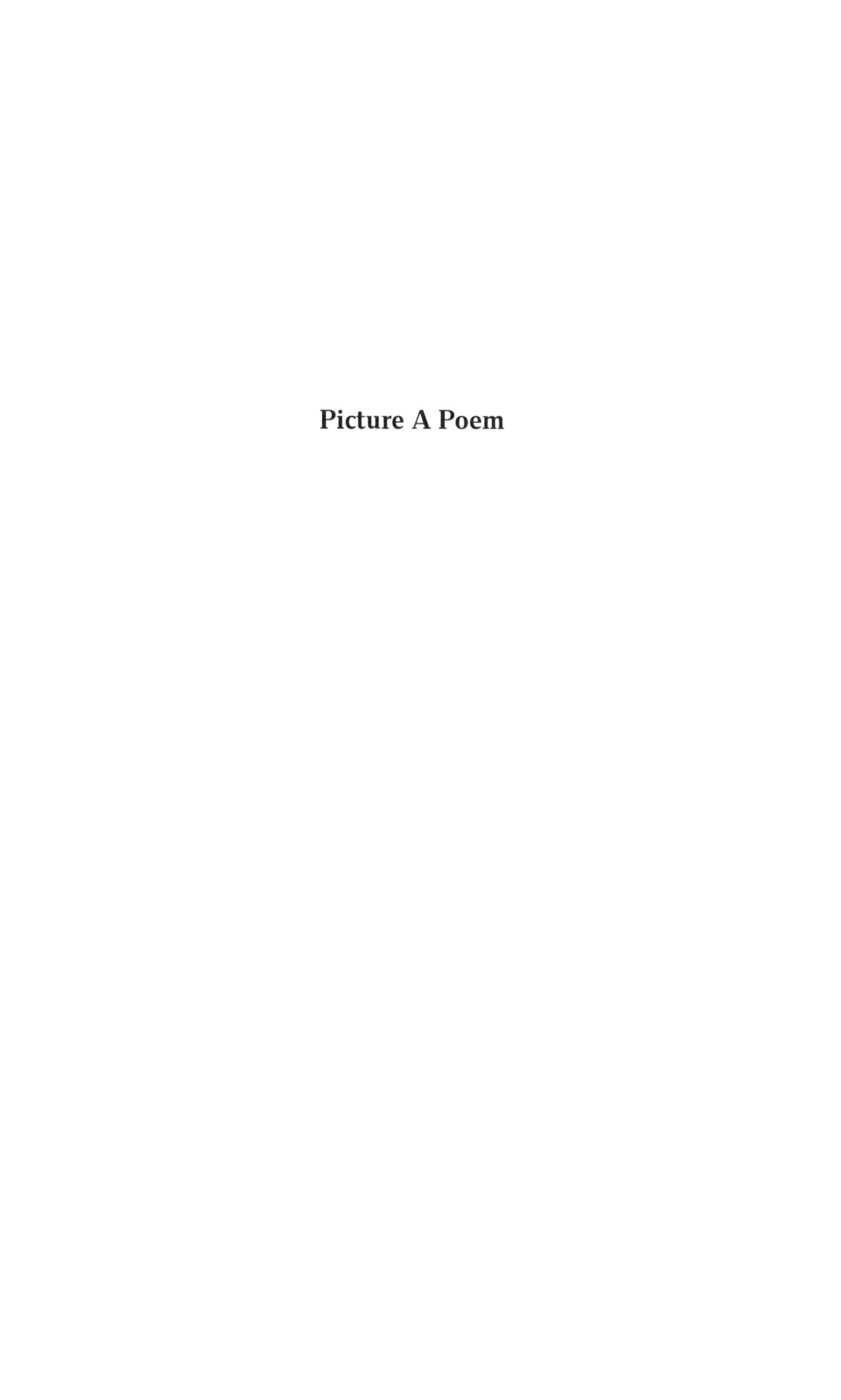

Picture A Poem

Also by
Caroline Giles Banks

Warm Under the Cat:
Haiku and Senryu Poems

The Clock Chimes:
Haiku and Senryu Poems

The Weight of Whiteness:
A Memoir in Poetry

The Clay Jar:
Haiku, Senryu and Haibun Poems

Tigers, Temples and Marigolds:
Haiku and Haibun Poems

PICTURE A POEM

Ekphrastic and Other Poems

by **Caroline Giles Banks**

WELLINGTON-GILES PRESS
Minneapolis, Minnesota
United States of America

WELLINGTON-GILES PRESS
4040 Sheridan Avenue South
Minneapolis, Minnesota 55410
United States of America
wellingtongilespress@gmail.com

Book design by Cate Hubbard

Library of Congress Control Number:
2014946793

ISBN 978-0-9645254-7-4
eBook ISBN 978-0-9645254-8-1

For
Patricia Hancock Wellington Giles
1921-1992

painter and poet

and for friends and family members
who also are writers and artists

Contents

I

II

Ekphrasis

a rhetorical device in which a visual object, such as a painting, photograph or sculpture, is described in words

I

View From Space

He thinks of a continent:
        the one seen in photos
        shot from the moon;
the one shaped like a heart;
the one where eons ago it all began;
        the one plundered
of our bodies, dreams, and gold;
        the one broken off,
        rifted from the rest;
the one where tears are immeasurable
as the Zambezi over Victoria Falls;
        the one where I am drowning
        and his shadow falls.

In Lascaux Cave

For T.S.H.

In my mind's eye
he comes to her
hunter fit erect naked
carrying a skull and spear.

He holds the bird bone over his face,
its large beak, like his phallus, pointing
to a bison bull transfixed by a spear.

From behind the mask his voice—
melodic,
rhythmic,
intimating a wish to protect, provide

if only he can touch
her soft skin—
seduces like one of Picasso's satyrs.

She asks him to hold still,
remove the mask. She wants
to capture his face, his magic, in paint.

But each violent sideways twist of his head,
mask firmly in place,
mocks her.

He leaps away
into the ochre, sienna, charcoal of memory.
Her crude sketch of
the faceless stickman

drawn millennia ago
on the rock cave wall
holds my gaze.

I try to remember
the color of my lover's eyes.

Venus Figure

Millennia ago a woman wishing
conception, a fecund legacy,
touched this small limestone figure,
its breasts swollen with anticipation,
magical triangle below the belly
full with child.

Today I stand in the gallery
where the figurine is displayed,
peering over the heads
of uniformed schoolchildren
swarming around her.
I will not speak
of her crumbling beauty,
the missing right breast,
the grumbling bellies
of too many children
outside in the streets,
the sad joy I feel
when I hold by infant grandson.
Isn't it enough to say
she fulfilled her promise?

Sphinx

Imagine the Sphinx—
    ancient creature
    with body of a lioness
    and human head.

Imagine when laurel crowned the head
    and made the lioness lie prone,
    turning her every move to stone.

Imagine when the lioness,
    wounded by this slight, severed herself
    from the head and was gone.

Imagine when the head, seeing herself
naked now below the neck,
bound up every human cell
    with notions of forever,
    foreignness and fame.

Imagine glimpsing the lioness
curled inside the belly
in a dream and sensing
    first joy and then
    pending calamity.

Imagine the primal pleasure of reunion,
only to wake and find the lioness,
like so many others,
    has almost disappeared.

Imagine the lioness.
Then try to answer
    Who am I?
without her   incomplete.

Female Shaman

Haniwa Figure

Tonight I guard the entry
to the museum gallery,
just as I stood sentry
in another kind of memorial
to revered leaders.
Around my neck I wear a talismanic amulet:
a fang, claw, beads of jade.
As my thick body loses
its waist, hips, and his desire,
I turn inward, drawing strength
from Kwannon Bosatsu's store.
In my right hand I offer up
to the goddess muse
a cup of jasmine and thyme
from the bag of curative herbs
wrapped around my wrist.
You have been patient.
You may now drink. Then,
when you look deeply,
my oval eyes and mouth will open
into the black well
of all mystery.

Group of Court Musicians

Three women kneel,
their small unglazed bodies
baked from clay.

Dull red paint fades on gauzy skirts
draped over their limbs, bent
in servitude for twelve centuries.

One leans forward extending a missing hand,
one stares stiffly ahead plucking a lute,
one turns a cheek ever so slightly to her flute.

The musicians are arranged around a small dog,
fired, like them,
in a perpetual sit-stay position,

unable to flee the regal gaze
of the upright empress
standing aloof and behind.

Today this courtly group is trapped
in a case of glass,
as inaccessible to the living

as it was when they played
underground for the dead
in sealed and guarded tombs.

Prajnaparamita, Goddess of Transcendental Wisdom

To you, my head seems perfection:

a little Buddha sits
at the base of the conical crown

and my mouth is finely chiseled
in an eternal smile.

Below the neck
I am crumbling.

One arm is broken
at the elbow,

the other severed
under the shoulder blade.

My missing limbs lie
far away underground.

If you look into my face
a mica tear

betrays my serenity
during centuries of plunder

that bring me here
before you.

Chou Tun-i Gazing Out Over Lotus

Chou Tun-i stares out
over the lotus pond
from his summer retreat
raised up on stilts
over the water's edge.
Hiding from the sun
under the ornate shelter's
roof and blinds,
he sits for hours at his desk,
the paper, brushes and ink
carefully arranged before him.
Lost in reverie
he does not see
the fisherman in his simple houseboat
moored nearby in the bamboo reeds,
his foot dangling in the water
while he plays his flute.

I want Chou Tun-i
to push back his chair,
stand up and turn away
from the paper, brushes and ink,
to step down from his retreat
and feel the muck and slime
of the long lotus roots
under his feet.

I want this for myself.

Poet with Birds

The massive white cloud pokes out
its head, shoulders, arm,

lifts the poet,
reflected in his reverie

in the meadow below,
up to the high notes

of white birds
perched in the red music tree,

his heavenly muse.

Quarrel

Red rage.
I left the bread cooling
in the cook shed

and surprised you
with my young niece
visiting from my brother's village. Now

our bed lies upside down,
its legs in the air, stiff,
a dead-dog marriage.

And the bloodied mattress, pad
of two deflowerings,
is my hard tomb, severed

where my head once lay
next to yours.
My hands,

black crows,
flap wildly
over your listless body,

carrion of betrayal.

Chagall Triptych

1

Lovers in the Lilacs

Unmoored from dirt, vase, hands,
pink and white lilacs
float above the horizon.
Fragrance balloons the bouquet
to dwarf the moon,
reduce the village to a spire.
A couple lies bedded
in this ether beyond
gravity.

2

L'Obsession

A crucifix crushes a Jew
holding three candles of death.
Skies stain red,
synagogues collapse in ashes.
Families pile into carts
harnessed to horses frozen
blue with shock.
Young wives wear widow's black,
barren by madness.

3

Couple on a Red Background

An acrobat balances
on the cock of a new day.
Rows of red houses corral
a white and green synagogue standing
whole on a hill.
Their bodies tethered to the ground,
a couple embraces in a golden meadow.
Pink and white lilacs float
in the cool blue pool of memory.
Here, palette and body are tempered twins,
the artist's hope for humankind
mature beyond division
or despair.

Questions for Diego Rivera, Painter of *Indian Spinning*

You paint her simple homespun dress
in pure white, clean
like the adobe wall she leans against.

You sit her on a flawless carpet
of bright mustard yellow.
Nearby, sticks are neatly bundled, tidy,

like the skein of wool she twists
between her fingers and toes,
her black braid. Diego,

why isn't she wearing
a shawl or hat
to ease the discomfort

of working outside midday?
Why isn't a colicky baby
strapped to her back,

or a toddler pulling her out
of her art? Diego,
whose utopia is this?

Did you idealize peasant life,
believe labor with the hands so noble
there could be no tatters,

chaos, dirt? Diego,
did she ever get to stand up
and walk out of your painting

to her life?

Harriet Tubman Series, No. 5

She felt the first sting of slavery when as a young girl she was struck on the head with an iron bar by an enraged overseer.

Jacob Lawrence

She is late
bringing water
to other field hands
working on Broadacres.
The buckets are so heavy,
backbreaking full.
One sharp blow to the left temple
knocks her to the ground,
banishing forever
the clear blue skies
and somersaults of girlhood.
Harriet sees two black trouser legs,
the overseer's rake-like arm
and hand—yellow-orange and grotesque—
tumble off the edge
of her field of vision.

The strike brings dreams
of leading others
towards the North Star's
light, away from the venom
of slavery.
Harriet leads hundreds of slaves
back and forth
over the demarcation line

to the promised land,
gains a bounty
in addition to the scar
on her head.

Nobody Around Here Calls Me Citizen

The blackest black man,
arms folded across
his shrunken chest
like the possibility of an equal sign,
stands before a wall
with the number ***2***
in red paint,
in my mind,
read to,
sign of the shuttered schools
of segregation.
A lion, tribal totem,
front paw and tail raised,
eyes piercing and mouth open,
ready to roar and strike,
shrinks inside the locked box of memory.

I want him
to put down his rake and hat,
to learn to read
about his roots in a continent
where mere centuries ago
his ancestors ruled kingdoms
and even lions were free,
to step to his left
and cover the number
until it
and all other rankings
are erased.

Fragments of Things

I often painted fragments of things
because it seemed to make my statement
as well as or better than the whole could.
Georgia O'Keeffe

1

Black Place III

A massive bolt of lightening splits
open the black-gray mountains
near Los Alamos.
Her eyes see
the blinding light, clouds of fire
coming over the mountains.
Her mind knows
the secret labs made a bomb
that surpasses the lightening's strike
to make the black place.

2

Pelvis IV

Still the war.
The morning moon,
blue sky,
are seen—like everything—
through bleached, dry bone.

3

January, 1944

Born
under the shadow
of the A-bomb, I learn
to seek shelter
under a desk, to fear
the black place,
fragments of things,
bone.

Dirty Little Secret

The machines sweep
their naked bodies,
lingering over armpits, upper lips,
radiating dreams
of easy, permanent beauty.

Using money earned from munitions factory jobs,
diverted from planting Victory gardens,
the women lie on cool, gray slabs
for the new, painless depilatory treatments.

They smile
as unwanted hair rubs off
on bath towels, underpants, bed sheets,
confirming fashion's dictate
to discard themselves.

Years later hard lumps poke
through the skin's surface,
sloughing off innocence
about X-ray technology,
the vulnerability of women

who, blind
as newborn marsupials,
desire
hairless bodies.

Fantastic Horse Cart

Italy, 1939.
She sits at the banquet table

about to marry
the town's rich, foolish, Fascist son.

The blue-faced fiddler, a Jew
besotted with her beauty,

flies his enormous one-eyed horse
and cart into the scene,

steals his beloved.
Before a full orange sun,

new morning moon,
the horse, jealous green,

embraces the fiddler and his love, carries them
from her youthful almost-mistake,

and lands them, their futures
together until death,

in a concentration camp.

Questions for Marisol, Sculptor of *The Cocktail Party*

1

Who Are They?

They are trustees, docents, donors,
rich enough,
to fund the wing
and hire the help
to serve the cocktails.

2

Why Did You Make Them Out of Wood?

I use hard woods, impenetrable,
dense and difficult
to topple. See how stiff,
blockish they are.
Each lacquered mask is interchangeable
with each ramrod body.

3

Why Is the Door Closed?

It is 1965. Detroit. Or Chicago.
Inner cities are on fire.
Blacks are rioting for deep changes,
equal accommodations,
for inclusion in an open
and Great Society.
There is resistance, fear
among those who have the most
to lose.

4

What Are They Talking About?

About golf scores, vacation plans,
dressmakers for altering
their floor-length, silk gowns,
about carpools, private schools
with tuitions high enough
to keep out the poor.

5

Does Making Art Sustain You?

My works can fit only
into gallery spaces,
require years, rare teaks and mahoganies.
I make ends meet
by waitressing.
The best jobs are fundraisers
and private parties at clubs.
I work the cocktail parties
to get the cash
to buy supplies.
After a few drinks
the guests give me
enormous tips,
whole stands of exotic trees
in 100 dollar bills.

6

Do You Think This Work Has Staying Power?

It is made to last.
The biggest threats
are fire and vandalism.
There is the remote possibility,
I suppose, that the security system
may be breeched, the figures damaged,
cut down, beheaded,
rearranged in radical ways:
the servants moved from the periphery
to the center, for instance.
But I'm sure the museum's board will see
that the assemblage remains
protected, preserved
without any changes.

Nightshade: a Study of the Simple, Practical and Amazing Potato

Fed up
with the glare of glitter,
the rickrack of excess,
and faux desires,
she turns her back
on sugarcoated gormandizing,
the drip-drop precision of monocropping,
and goes underground
to inhabit the dark cell.
She sits alone
at the plain wood table
for her one daily meal, imbibing
the damp discipline of denial.
Convent-trained, she holds the fork
with the tines turned down,
begins her slow devotional
of cut, pause, and chew.
Finished with her simple supper,
a potato,
she lays the fork over
the knife in a cross,
and meditates
on the plight of peasants,
the persistent famine,
without and
within.

There is No Fat in Heaven

In a paper grocery bag
she places torn images
of her mother,
the photos she took of her
in the casket at the funeral.
Peelings of still-fragrant orange,
pores oozing shining droplets of oil,
mix with her mother's body
in the bottom of the sack.
It's all garbage now, she thinks,
as she tosses her dead mother's body
and the husk of her only meal for the day
into the trash.

Hungering for something beyond flesh,
beyond desire,
in the cache of denial,
she starves.
No food, no flesh, no fat.
Look at me, her thinness says,
I live on nothing but faith,
holy, like the saints before me.
Negation of gravity,
she floats,
all light,
pure spirit,
raptured to heaven
to reunite with the one
who has gone before.

Vanitas: Flesh Dress for an Albino Anorectic

For Lady Gaga, who wore this dress

I watch you jogging
trying to keep your pale body
haute couture thin.
I will make a dress
to stop you,
turn you around.

The mannequin is like you: armless, legless,
just a torso
covered with a fine soft fabric skin.
A small wooden knob protrudes
between the shoulders for the head, a stick
like the figure you want.

The gown puts some weight, some meat
back on your body.
Patches of raw flank steak,
bloody and pliable like you were, newly born,
are sutured with thread
to make thick, raised scar seams
between the breasts,
across the belly and back.
I salt the dress
to preserve it,
make it tougher.
Over time the muscles harden,
pull and tear the fat
into lacy webs and striations.

Dark bruises blotch
the right breast and hip, the left thigh.
The flesh droops and sags,
stiffens into deep folds
as it ages.

As you wear this flesh dress, think
on the ways of fashion, the body,
like the 17th century Dutch who pondered
the human skull, the rotting pheasant or hare
portrayed in the still life compositions
after which I name your gown.

Without Words

I'm going away, leaving
my body,
his thick wool overcoat
behind in the tall dry grass.

When the coat swoops
close and opens wide
I split off my mouth,
making a jagged break

just above the upper lip.
Beads of spittle travel
along the mouth seam
clenched hard as white marble.

Its cries can't reach my ears.
I vacate my skinny torso.
It steps aside
and turns its back

on the dark overcoat.
Its legs weld together, tight
as cooled bronze.

What is left of *I*
hides in a place
the coat can't find.

Three geese rise
from a patch
of tall dry grass

and meld
into the gray-blue sky.

Georgia O'Keeffe, a Portrait

Fiddlehead ferns unfolding
to a posed domesticity,
her fingers, long and delicate,
shuck an ear of corn,
darn dark velvet.
Her hands touch
a sheer kimono,
her breasts, caress
a shiny new hubcap,
steering wheel,
one of her skulls.
Her paintings—
the ones we now know
petal-by-petal—
are mere backdrops
for her husband's
black palladium portraits
of her head and hands.

She Was Tired of Filling Her Heart with Hopeless Dreams

Wind slaps open
the window of her heart,
shredding the veil
between inside and out.
She was tired
of filling it
with hopeless dreams.
She slashes at its walls,
tearing the pink skin.
She smashes the mirror
of her vanity, its images
of long strapless gowns
for fairy-tale balls.
Shards of broken glass lie
beside a high-heeled slipper, hairbrush,
ripped pages of a diary.
                A goddess,
ancient and regal,
stands still in a corner,
aloof and impervious to her rage.
Her lamp shines
on the destruction,
its beam touching
that awful space
between hope and its betrayal,
refusing her heart
to let it go.

Relative Perfection

1

Vanilla Geyser

Wedding dresses
dangle out of reach, suspended
from Big Dipper-sized dreams.
A vanilla breeze wafts up
from a mountain of cakes,
stirring the tulle petticoats
with their crystal drops.

I once had a bride doll
with a dress like these.
I saw her in a glass case at FAO Schwarz
and begged to have her
for my birthday.
She was yanked from my hands
and disappeared
when I talked back
to my mother.

2

Looking Glass Pictures

Around gray padded walls
of an octagonal room, dark
as an asylum for hysterics,
black-and-white photos
of women stare
through a grid of shadows.
They ended up here
because they wanted more
than they got.
I recognize an older woman
as the waitress in the café
who serves rich chocolate cake
to women like me
when we're blue-hungry
and have forgotten why.

3

Guardian Angels: Some Invented Families in Late 20th Century North America

Studio portraits of women
celebrating their families
hang outside the gray padded room.
Two women and their son
smile before a JCPenny blue cloth sky.
A dark-skinned boy leans
into his pink mother's lap.
She says a family is
people who love each other
during the good/bad times in life.
For her birthday she wants
a factory-made layer cake
with lard and sugar frosting,
roses, and her name in blue.
She will pick one up,
and a lottery ticket,
at SUPERAMERICA on her way
home from work.
They will eat cake, watch TV,
and make a wish to win
the big prize next time.

4

My Infant Grandson

sits on my lap.
I have turned my house over
to my young son
and younger daughter-in-law
and retreated to the basement.
Tucked in the back corner
of my closet I keep
a long simple gown
with satin ribbon,
yellowed now
and much too small,
bought years ago
to wear someday
with a man I love.
It haunts me,
the ghost
of my missing bride doll.

Mother and Child

20th Century Yombe
(Democratic Republic of Congo)

My boy-child lies on my lap.
His head, resting in the palm of my left hand,
turns from my pendulous breasts.

Before fleeing the fighting
we sat on the earthen graves
of our Yombe ancestors,
bringing fertility and honor
to our clan. Here,

in a sealed box of metal and glass,
we sit alone before you.
The air grows stale and
I am afraid.

I wear all my power
to keep alive the link
between Yombe past
and Yombe future:

a necklace of six canine teeth,
black spots on my orange-brown body,
a blacker tattoo in the small of my back.

But I am terrified
this will not be enough
to make you hear my cries
for my limp boy-child.

Les Charmes du Paysage

(The Delights of Landscape)

A rifle leans on red pigment
outside an empty picture frame,
firing the imagination
to fill the void
with death from the countryside.

I imagine a soft platinum hare,
profiled eye drained of light,
suspended upside down
for the center scene, or

a pheasant's iridescent plumage
waiting to be plucked,
waiting to be a bird
of gastronomical use
after its painted image dries.

The gun barrel's brush on canvas
shatters a doe's reverie,
alerting her to leap
out of art
towards the safety
of unrepresented light.

Toppling Saddam

April 9, 2003

Baghdad.
The young marine
shimmies up Saddam,
blindfolds him
with an American flag.

After the dictator is toppled
by the tank's lassoed noose,
Iraqi boys scurry
from the crowd to beat
the bronze behemoth
with the soles of their sandals,
counting coup
with leather and rubber.

Their fathers, faces alternating awe
and fear of reprisal
for these slaps of disrespect,
call their sons back
to remnants of boyhood. And

the G.I., too caught up
in the game
to think
about the press,
hears his commander,
removes the star-spangled hangman's hood,

jumps down to political correctness:
the U.S. is here to liberate, not
conquer the Iraqis.

Continents away we watch
the drumroll of this scene shot
through camera lenses
embedded in tanks—old animosities
delivered in new, real time—
hoodwinked into believing
the swift destruction of a public statue
is the end
of a dictator.

Letters From the People

the curvaceous buttocks
of the brassy ***3***
hangs loose on the front stoop

the peeling ***&***
tires
of holding words together

TV kills

the repetitive betrayal of names
Wayne and Katie
Wayne and Jan
written in the same hand

God Is Man

the confusion and fatigue of words
closed rests on ***open***
in the shop window

K straddles the barbed wire fence
a prisoner   hesitant
to escape   or stay

Where is Richie?

the dripping white ***C***
lets go
unable to hold itself together

the photographer's un-cropped reflection
defies directives in ***No Posting***
fixes their howls   ***terrible***   in emulsion

II

She Arrived Like a Long-Lost Cousin

She arrived like a long-lost cousin:
uninvited, bold
in her claim for accommodation.
I tried to ignore her.
I even hid.
I had other things to do.
Still, she keeps coming back, insistent
like the Witnesses who work my block.

I give a little. A few hours
on Saturday mornings. Greedy
for expression, for *life*,
she bustles right in with an outfit
from the costume room
of a Shakespearean playhouse: a crown
and floor-length cloak. Sometimes
the capelet sits easy
on the shoulders, a kid's play towel
safety-pinned around the neck. Sometimes
it is heavy, a peacock-feathered robe
weighted with stuff caught
in deep troll.

She has traveled through space and time.
She speaks with the measured pain
of a runaway on the Underground Railroad,
with the elegance and deceiving simplicity
of the counted, syllabic haiku,
with Irish wit and tenor, and Teutonic bore.

We are getting used to each other. Sometimes
we walk posture-perfect,
finishing school girls practicing
on the pageant runway. Sometimes
we just clown around, or drowse.
I am working her into my routine.
I have cleared space in the guestroom closet
and asked her to unpack her things.
She hasn't said how long she'll stay.

Dream Fragments

1

I'm in a place
that might be the sanatorium
in Mann's *Magic Mountain*.
It is grand, expansive in scale.
Windows lead the eye out
to manicured lawns, a lake,
gray mountains in the distance.
                                        Inside
gurneys, strewn about at odd
and disordered angles,
lie empty.
Steel side-bars are snapped up,
cold arms readied to grip
a body and make it infantile.
On white sheets
stains of brown blood and grime
make outlines of figures,
faded selves once sketched
then discarded, or outgrown.
                                        Alone,
except for the usual
and vaguely discernable companions,
I stand under a mobile
of a dozen paper figures dangling
around a small and deflated globe
and wonder how I ended up here,
why no one comes
to care
for us.

2

He comes
down a street
carrying rocks.
At first
I see only
the rocks,
how beautiful,
pinkish-gray,
well-matched in size
they are.
Then I notice the color/mood of time:
it is summer,
dark.
It has just rained. Now
he is a man
I once loved
dressed in a straw Stetson hat
and blue-and-white seersucker suit.

We stroll together,
his arm around my silhouetted shoulders,
heading towards
an open-air theater
where an ancient drama
is about to begin.
Over the low split rail fence
running along the ravine
between us
I say,
Don't make it too difficult for me.

I cannot tell him
I'm in a somnolent place
where lives are partial outlines.
With lights dimming
and a dry ice fog seeping up around me
he is gone.

3

I enter a cathedral
carrying a nest of empty boxes.
I am younger.
The earth is still soft beneath my feet.
I walk up and down the aisles looking
for a seat, my life, my lover
but there is no place for me.
                                        Wounded,
I retreat to an annex
and sleep for years
face down on a bed,
arms spread to the side.

Tonight I stand outside that cathedral.
Rolls of carpeting anticipate
an otherworldly union.
The carpet is white
and lies between
where I've come from,
where I want to be.
                                        I pause.
I am older, afraid
to approach it,
that it will disappoint,
disappear.
                                        I want
to hover just above the surface, suspended,
the way I've moved before
at night with mythic fleetness.

How long will I resist
that small voice from below?

let go
come down
touch me

Gifts

Inside the palace,
magnificent and ornate,
women wait
to go up
the wide circular staircase
to a throne of dark, rich mahogany.
Each cradles in her hands,
outstretched in offering,
lyric poems,
or plays in progress,
novels, first or last,
learned essays.
Each crosses to the throne,
assumes the mantel and crown,
transformed
by her gifts.

A Riddle Dream

I am in Italy, in Rome, alone.
I can tell it is Rome
by the postcard horizon
of spires and domes.

I crouch, curl, slide out headfirst
from a tight, dark passage,
assisted by a man.
I step out, shining, shimmering

wet, wearing a long white gown,
sheer, silk, the kind
kept in the back
of a drawer for a wedding night.

I say, *I have to find,*
I'm looking for
Regina, a museum.
Regina, Latin for *queen,*

the peacocked-feathered one,
jealous consort, foreboder,
ancient as myth. I find
she is hidden in the museum,

in the word,
not the place.

An Angel Before

A dimple in the back
of each shoulder.
Her mother said
and the girl believed her
each spot marked
where a wing used to be.
What an odd twist
to have been
an angel before,
before being a daughter,
the wings clipped, ripped,
torn, removed
by her mother's giving birth.

Dear Meridel,

I remember,
clear as a snapshot,
dropping by your home one evening,

seeing you
through the window
reading Gertrude Stein.

We walked out
into the backyard,
the soft air,
and coming back
into the kitchen

you pulled
a handful of leaves
from a tree

and dropped them
into a kettle of soup
as we passed the stove.

You
were
the
first
eagle
I
knew.

The Body is Nothing

Margaret's garbage for one day: one onion skin, grape stems,
a banana peel, one egg shell, one empty can of green beans.
Estimated calories consumed: less than 500.

We had the most marvelous family life
that it was almost unreal.

Dad was an old-fashioned father.
He always disciplined and, boy, his word was....
You just obeyed. You did it,
or else. He read the Bible to us,
a wonderful, wonderful Christian person.

Mother tested recipes for Betty Crocker.
The picture is the all-American family....
She'd take those little willow sticks
and whip our legs with them.

I get my dinner all set,
take a bath, get spotlessly clean.
I eat half my meal
and then I take a bath
halfway through my dinner
so I feel all fresh again.
Then before I hop into bed
I take another bath so I feel
immaculately fresh.

The body is nothing.
Anybody who believes in the Bible
would believe in that
as a matter of fact.
For me, it's a way of life,
my whole self, really.
That's why I can't think of it
as a disease
or anything,
you know
.

Ode to Number Three

The triptych,
object of adoration's genuflect,
opens its hinged wings
to halos' golden rings
over attendants
to right and left
of the holy child. And

the ménage à trois,
threesomes of empires'
and households' demise,
literature's and art's surprise:
Bloomsbury threes,
Woolfs howling down
each other's sanity.
In Drabble's *Companion*:
D'Artagnon and his *Three Musketeers*,
Brecht's *Threepenny Opera*,
Trollope's *Three Clerks*.

And in social philosophy
cycles of threes
seed cyclones
of revolutions,
some now dashed
by fumbling,
corruption,
cold wars.

Even animals
are granted
the cardinal three:
the Triple Crown's
horseshoe garland
guarantees the victor
years of siring offspring.

Years ago
a psychic saw
three children:
one son,
one grandson,
one granddaughter.
I am complete.

Ode to Three Pillows

Simply fashioned
out of the root of a tree,
the nomad's pillow:
portable plant, portable past
for the man or woman
who travels in life
as well as in dreams.
Tossed out,
too cumbersome to carry,
it is now an exotic item,
collected, inventoried, encased.

On the soft one of airy down
plucked from his paddocked, wing-clipped friends,
fence-bound peasant
dreams of multiplying flocks.
He puts his head on
the dividend of his dinner,
their necks wrung so his can rest.

The modern dreamer, city slicker,
puts her head on synthetic stuff
at the end of the day.
Without so much as a human touch
it reshapes itself each morning,
impervious to individual shape and form.
Progress, the tag proclaims: dust-free, dander-free,
antiseptic of animal and earth.

I, too, dream the dreams of wanderers,
traversing all lands, even skies, in sleep.
I, too, dream the dreams of peasants,
or at least count sheep.
I, too, dream the dreams of city slickers.
I have put my head to all three.

Lessons in Bipedalism

After a sedentary day teaching
students about human origins, gatherers
and hunters in millennia

and continents only imagined,
I walk the campus path,
my high cholesterol count

and extra fat on my mind.
The path is a product
of immigrants' sensible forethought:

planned, purely recreational, groomed,
now signed a one-way street.

Driving home on the highway,
miles from the campus path, I see suddenly
a man walking along the freeway.

He wears a suit, dark, wool, thick.
He is not out of gas or walking away
from car trouble. His stride says

he is going to work, to market, perhaps
to visit kin. I imagine
he walked away from a burning

Soweto township—the list of possibilities
is endless—or a prison cell, and kept on
walking in and out of languages,

dialects, currencies, markets (black
and not black), political ideologies,
mastering them all,
not for a paper-pencil exam,
but for his life.

Across oceans and continents he steps
into my mindscape, walks circles around me
with my learnedness about
the relation between posture
and survival.

Boys Prepare for Life

Summer afternoon.
Two boys run along the lakeshore.
In masks, snorkels and fins
they are amphibious, quasi-terrestrial,
half in, half out of it.

One says, *we are mission men,*
men on a mission.
The other, without a pause,
no, we are gods.
Easy as jumping off the high board
they set their standards high, moon
the mundane, soar up
into the sublime.

Cross-Country Skiing: Grand Portage, Minnesota

A long steep ascent
from the lakeshore.
On a snowy hill
overlooking Lake Superior
my skis leave
fossil-like impressions,
vestigial vertebrae
of some giant Lake Dweller,
now extinct.

Tired and lost,
wanting a place to rest
and, finally, to stop,
I stick one pole in the snow
like the sharp point
of a grade school compass, then
extend the other to the horizon line
to make an arc.
Spinning it quickly
to complete the circle,
it encompasses the globe
and brings me back again.

Hiking in the Shenandoah

Alone at the bottom of the valley,
midpoint of the day,
midpoint of my life,
I begin the steep ascent.

Soon my muscles burn,
fingers tingle and swell,
eyes star, the universe whirls.
Collapsed on a rock

I freeze, then melt
blood, sweat, tears.
Thoughts surface: I do not want to die.
Vows surface: to give myself away.

To lighten the load
on the way up
I drop first
egoism

then narcissism,
stoicism,
patriotism,
even humanism,

ism
after
ism.
I reach the top

with simply this:
from now on
I will hold on
to a hand.

An Occasional Cup of Coffee

It is July 10th 1990. It is early evening.
I step outside into my neighborhood
and find things I did not know I loved,
my son's high-top sneakers,
two-toned and garish, a size eleven.
I want to bronze these smelly high tops
and dangle them like dice
from my car mirror,
a bid against
the wrench and grief of impending loss.

Delicate sparrows dart in and out
of the opening in my rotting porch roof.
We are co-tenants in this niche
of Linden Hills. I think about
letting the porch go one more year
and giving the birds the other rooms,
one by one.

I turn the corner past
my neighbor's house, a man
I have loved for many years.
It is a love not unrequited,
only circumscribed by decisions, commitments,
cowardice. We settle for cups of coffee
and talk at the local café.
I have learned to love
an occasional cup of coffee.

And words, simple words, like *STOP,*
GO SLOW, YIELD, DO NOT ENTER,
words which point to limitations
and made me mad,
now roll off my back like water.
Until tonight I did not know
I loved these words.

Intermission at the Bolshoi Opera, Moscow

For G.H.

When he, mere mortal,
teases me
during intermission
about romance
and the longing of lovers
in *Prince Igor*,
SHE, mad as Callas could be,
appears on cue,
her long black cape swirling,
and trills in her loudest,
most wounded voice:
Watch your tone.

Air Mattress

For H.I.

He pulls in
little gasps of air,
practiced,
not like a man

close to drowning,
puffs each breath
into the tube
to make a bed.

I sleep
on his capped breath.
In the morning,
kneeling to open the stop,

he extends
his chest, arms, head
over the mattress, and,
pressing his hands

along the pillow's rounded ridges,
releases his breath
in one Neptunian exhale,
blowing a lost boat

home to harbor.

On a Night

Funereal crows mark the place
where red smears cross
the asphalt to deer carcasses,
white undersides belly up,
struck in night blindness.

My son is driving now
and making me crazy.
He goes too fast
on icy streets. I yell, *slow down,*
slow down, damn it!
I don't want to die.
There! I've said it. He made me say
what has been bugging me all along.
Pounding the dash with my fist, hard,
to break the words open, on a night
like so many other winter nights,
I think of the deer and the crows
and start to make the trip
to home.

Paper, Scissors, Rock

The world is suddenly different.
Headlines declare, *War in the Persian Gulf.*
Stunned by this national stutter
of WAR, WAR, WAR, I go outside
to walk off the buzz:
too much live coverage,
too little sleep.

I call it the Peace Garden.
By the side of the path
three evergreens witness
my grief, my solitude.
Branches uplifted, they are three Fates,
multi-armed bodhisattvas. I,
the one with words, tell them
I will not be silenced. I will
use my mouth, my pen, this paper,
a gift from you, sister trees,
to insist that other words
be spoken: PEACE
and PEACE again,
and PEACE.

Thinking Twice

This time we come through the stiles
with designer-label tie-dyes,
cell phones, sobering mortgages and IRAs—
no, not Irish armies, just retirements—
on our minds.

Dylan returns
to old ballads and tunes
with his funky harmonica wail:
Like a Rolling Stone, It Ain't Me Babe,
I Want You.

But this is no song-along.
Dylan teases.
We are playing in new tempos and times.
What have I done for the homeless, the poor,
the threat of thermonuclear war?

Don't Think Twice,
It's All Right.

For the Dancer Mikhail Baryshnikov in Kafka's *Metamorphosis*

Any of various oval, flat-bodied insects
of the family Blattidae,
several species of which are common
household pests. Also called 'roach.'

Across the linoleum table top
las cucarachas samba and tango
Woodstock style: frenzied,
without partner, fickle,
scattering like mute teenagers
with light after the last dance.

Freak accident: man falls backwards
down kingdom to class,
family to phylum,
genus to species, and
lands encased in body of bug.
Shunted to floorboard perspective
he is all legs, torso and wing.
No prologue, no monologue, no dialogue.
Pure motion, scurry and leap.

Hiroshima Remembrance

In a flash the slow irreplaceable weave
of millennia unravels.

Kafka's *Metamorphosis,* a prophesy of sorts:
cockroaches, suddenly now graced, move up

the ladder while other earthbound creatures,
disbelieving, free-fall

from their kingdoms, classes, families, and
phyla into radiated oblivion. I believe

a mere one hundred Hiroshimas can cancel
all futures, all pasts.

III

HAIKU

realtor's office
leaves yellow
on the money tree

opening up
in the therapist's garden
bleeding hearts

federal sequester
only one rose
at the MLK Memorial

Little League baseball
the carillon of
metal bats

State
Fair
the
toddler
asks
if
the
winding
entry
ramp
is
a
ride

Harvard '58
still placing silver
in his blazer's breast pocket

returning
the blood diamond
broken dreams

hearing aids
for the first time
the jangle of earrings

shoulder dimples
spots where her wings
used to be

brain MRI
trying to recall everything
on my bucket list

opening the report
on the neuropsych exam
whiteout

approaching hospice
the car at the intersection
reads URN

counting open lids
on the pill box
it's Wednesday

Water, Wind, Fire:
Japan Earthquake and Tsunami

1

Water

the Pacific Ocean
destroys, then cools
the reactors

reactor meltdown
temp workers scrub walls
with brushes and rags

adrift at sea
for three weeks
his wagging tail

evacuation map
fish crisscross
under the *hot* zone

pausing over the menu
not ordering
sushi

temple ablutions
rinsing each hand
but not the mouth

tea ceremony
the honored guest
moved to tears
San Diego, CA

2

Wind

aftershocks
even the clouds
move differently

aftershocks
so many
haiku

no man is an....
radiation levels spike
in LA

ban on planting rice
empty fields
empty bowls

milk safety check
the cow chews her cud
in sync with the Geiger counter

imported soy sauce
checking the label
for the manufacture date

3

Fire

meal time
survivors fire grills
with walls and floors

avoiding *pan-ku*
workers hide burns
with flesh-colored bandages

Prius spare parts
indefinitely
on back order

photo albums
pulling memories
from the rubble

India 2013

bull's-eye
the farmer's red turban
in the mustard field

multicolored saris
in the tea plantation
special harvest blend

silky tassels
green and gold saris shimmer
in fields of maize

unable to climb
all the temple stairs
resting in limbo

Ayurvedic spa
a cow's moo
ends meditation

shuttered factory
the workers' faded poster—
Be an Optimist

celebrity
all the diners hold up
menus   and iPads

Park for World Unity
permission to enter
delayed

Fodor's Choice hotel
5 stars   and billy clubs
keep out the unwanted

India independence
royal palaces
now in hotel chains

pilgrims on smartphones
tweeting and twittering
enlightenment

released from my vows
water from the sacred river
wets my face

Notes

Listed below are the titles, artists and dates of the works of art upon which the ekphrastic poems in Section I are based. **Images of these works of art can be found online by searching for the artist, title, date and location of the work.** Poems awarded prizes are also noted.

Page 1: "View From Space,"
NASA, Apollo 8, image of 'Earthrise,' 1968.

Page 2: "In Lascaux Cave,"
Lascaux, a cave in southwest France, contains stunning Paleolithic paintings.

Page 4: "Venus Figure,"
about 20,000 B.C. Paleolithic (probably La Mouthe, France).
Minneapolis Institute of Arts, Minneapolis, Minnesota.

Page 5: "Sphinx,"
The Sphinx is a figure in Egyptian and Greek myth having the body of a lion and the head of a man or woman.

Page 7: "Female Shaman,"
6th century Japan.
Minneapolis Institute of Arts, Minneapolis, Minnesota.

Page 8: "Group of Court Musicians,"
early 8th century China.
Minneapolis Institute of Arts, Minneapolis, Minnesota.

Page 9: "Prajnaparamita, Goddess of Transcendental Wisdom,"
13th century Cambodia.
Minneapolis Institute of Arts, Minneapolis, Minnesota.

Page 10: "Chou Tun-i Gazing Out Over Lotus,"
Liu Chun, @1500 China.
Minneapolis Institute of Arts, Minneapolis, Minnesota.

Page 11: "Poet with Birds,"
Marc Chagall, 1911.
Minneapolis Institute of Arts, Minneapolis, Minnesota.

Page 12: "Quarrel,"
Marc Chagall, 1914.

Page 13: "Lovers in the Lilacs,"
Marc Chagall, 1930.

Page 14: "L'Obsession,"
Marc Chagall, 1943.

Page 15: "Couple on a Red Background,"
Marc Chagall, 1983.

Page 16: "Questions for Diego Rivera, Painter of *Indian Spinning*,"
"Indian Spinning,"
Diego Rivera, 1936.

Page 18: "Harriet Tubman Series, No. 5,"
Jacob Lawrence, 1939-1940.

This is the fifth of the 31-panel Harriet Tubman Series, narrative paintings by Jacob Lawrence. Lawrence 'tells stories' in his work, primarily about African American history and social justice. He researched Tubman's life and wrote the captions that accompany the paintings. While my poem is inspired by painting No. 5, it makes reference to the entire Tubman series.

Page 20: "Nobody Around Here Calls Me Citizen,"
Robert Gwathmey, 1943.
Weisman Art Museum,
the University of Minnesota, Minneapolis, Minnesota.

Page 21: "Black Place III,"
Georgia O'Keeffe, 1944.

Page 22: "Pelvis IV,"
Georgia O'Keeffe, 1944.

Page 24: "Dirty Little Secret,"
Erica Spitzer Rasmussen, 2000.
Mixed media with handmade paper.

Page 25: "Fantastic Horse Cart,"
Marc Chagall, 1949.

The film, *Life is Beautiful,* is set in 1939 Italy. In viewing the film I saw Chagall's painting, *Fantastic Horse Cart,* enacted in the scene where Dora, engaged to the village's foolish, Fascist, and arrogant clerk, is stolen from her engagement party by Guido, who is Jewish. He rides a green horse covered with anti-Semitic slogans into the party and carries Dora off to their life together: marriage, parenthood, internment and death in a concentration camp. The 1997 film, directed by and starring Roberto Benigni, won three Academy Awards.

Page 26: "Questions for Marisol, Sculptor of *The Cocktail Party,*"
"The Cocktail Party,"
Marisol, 1965–66.

Page 30: "Nightshade: a Study of the Simple, Practical, and Amazing Potato,"
Krista Kelly Walsh. Art in Space XII, Part One, 1998.
Intermedia Arts, Minneapolis, Minnesota.
*** The poem won First Prize, 20th Annual St. Paul AAUW Poetry Contest, 1999.

Page 31: "There Is No Fat in Heaven,"
This poem is based on my doctoral research on religious beliefs about food and the body in the subjective experiences of women with the eating disorder, anorexia nervosa. For additional information on my research see the following publications:
Caroline Giles Banks, " 'Culture' in Culture-Bound Syndromes: the Case of Anorexia Nervosa", *Social Science and Medicine, an international journal* 34, no. 8 (April 1992);
________," 'There is No Fat in Heaven': Religious Asceticism and the Meaning of Anorexia Nervosa," *Ethos* 24, no. 1 (March 1996);
________," The Imaginative Use of Religious Symbols in Subjective Experiences of Anorexia Nervosa," *The Psychoanalytic Review* 84, no. 2 (April 1997);
________,"Illness Narratives and Human Development: Changing Metaphors about the Body in a Case of Anorexia Nervosa," *Cultural Studies: A Research Volume* 3, ed. Norman Denzin. Stanford, Conn. and London, England: JAI Press, Inc., 1998.

Page 32: "Vanitas: Flesh Dress for an Albino Anorectic,"
Jana Sterbak, 1998.
Exhibited at the Walker Art Center, Minneapolis, Minnesota.

Page 34: "Without Words,"
Judith Shea, 1988.
Minneapolis Sculpture Garden, Minneapolis, Minnesota.

Page 36: "Georgia O'Keeffe, A Portrait,"
Alfred Stieglitz. New York, NY:
The Metropolitan Museum of Art, 1978.

Page 37: "She Was Tired of Filling Her Heart with Hopeless Dreams,"
Hollis Sigler, 1982.

Page 38: "Vanilla Geyser,"
Cynthia Morgan, 1998.
A mixed media installation at the Minneapolis Institute of Arts,
Minneapolis, Minnesota, Summer 1998.

Page 39: "Looking Glass Pictures,"
Barbara Nei, 1997-98.
A mixed media installation at the Minneapolis Institute of Arts,
Minneapolis, Minnesota, Summer 1998.

Page 40: "Guardian Angels: Some Invented Families in Late 20th
Century North America,"
Leigh Kane, 1994-2000.
A mixed media installation at the Minneapolis Institute of Arts,
Minneapolis, Minnesota, Summer 1998.

Page 42: "Mother and Child,"
20th century Yombe, Democratic Republic of Congo.
Minneapolis Institute of Arts, Minneapolis, Minnesota.

Page 43: "Les Charmes du Paysage,"
Magritte, 1928.

Page 46: "Letters From the People,"
photos from *Letters From the People*,
Lee Friedlander. New York, NY: D.A.P., 1993.

Page 51: "She Arrived Like a Long-Lost Cousin,"
*** Winner, Me and My Angel Poetry Contest, 1996.

Page 60: "An Angel Before,"
***Winner, Me and My Angel Poetry Contest, 1996.

Page 61: "Dear Meridel,"
A 'found poem' in the form of a letter to Meridel Le Sueur inserted in one of her books in the Meridel Le Sueur Collection at Augsburg College, Minneapolis, Minnesota.

Page 66: "Ode to Three Pillows,"
*** Honorable mention, Anthropology and Humanism Poetry Contest, 1990.

In the early 1980s while visiting the Samburu, seminomadic pastoralists in northern Kenya, I came across a headrest made out of the root of a tree which had been discarded, most likely because it was riddled with bugs. I got to thinking about the relation of the simple pillow to other aspects of culture, such as subsistence bases and notions of self and personhood. In the poem I consider, in turn, nomadic cultures, agriculturally based peasant cultures and cultures dependent on the use of concentrated fossil fuels and related materials. The third stanza of the poem implies a critical bias of modern culture against the 'dust and dander' of traditional cultures. The voice of the anthropologist/poet in stanza four suggests that I/we are potential brokers across cultures. Caroline Giles Banks, *Anthropology and Humanism Quarterly* 15, no. 4 (December 1990).

Page 68: "Lessons in Bipedalism,"
***Honorable Mention, Anthropology and Humanism Poetry Contest, 1991.

The very title of Caroline G. Banks's 'Lessons in Bipedalism' suggests that the learned observer in the poem is going to have an uncomfortable (albeit enriching) experience of some kind; Banks's sensitive distinction between walking for mere good health and walking for survival is, indeed, a telling lesson.
David Kirby, *Anthropology and Humanism Quarterly* 16, no. 4 (December 1991).

Page 74: "An Occasional Cup of Coffee,"
***2nd Prize, 19th Annual St. Paul AAUW Poetry Contest, 1998.

Page 82: "Hiroshima Remembrance,"
Read at the 50th Anniversary Observance, August 6, 1995, Lake Harriet Rock Garden, Minneapolis, Minnesota.

Page 91: "Water, Wind, Fire: Japan Earthquake and Tsunami,"
In March 2011 a 9.0 magnitude earthquake took place northeast of Tokyo. It resulted in a series of catastrophic nuclear emergencies at the Fukushima Daiichi and Daini nuclear power plants.

Page 96: "India 2013,"
These haiku are from *Tigers, Temples and Marigolds: Haiku and Haibun Poems*, Caroline Giles Banks. Minneapolis, MN: Wellington-Giles Press, 2013.

Acknowledgements

The author would like to acknowledge the editors of the following anthologies, journals and magazines for publishing the poems listed below, some in slightly modified form.

Caroline Giles Banks, "View From Space," *Imagination and Place/ Cartography*, ed. Kelly Barth. Lawrence, Kansas: Imagination and Place Press, 2013. Also in *Full Circle* 27, ed. Leon Knight. Robbinsdale, MN: Guild Press, 2006.

________, "In Lascaux Cave," *Sidewalks, An Anthology of Poetry, Short Prose and Art*, no. 16, ed. Tom Heie. Champlin, MN: Sidewalks, Spring/Summer 1999. Also in *Anthropology and Humanism* 24, no. 2 (December 1999).

________, "Venus Figure," *Anthropology and Humanism* 24, no.2 (December 1999). Also in *Re-Imagining, Quarterly Publication of the Re-Imagining Community/ Re-imagining Feminism,* no. 16 (February 1999).

________, "Sphinx," *Full Circle Twenty*, ed. Leon Knight. Robbinsdale, MN: Guild Press, 1999. Also in *Forced From the Garden: Poetry and Short Prose by Women*, ed. Ginny Knight. Robbinsdale, MN: Guild Press, 2003.

________, "Female Shaman," *Re-Imagining, Quarterly Publication of the Re-imagining Community/ Re-imagining Feminism,* no. 16 (February 1999).

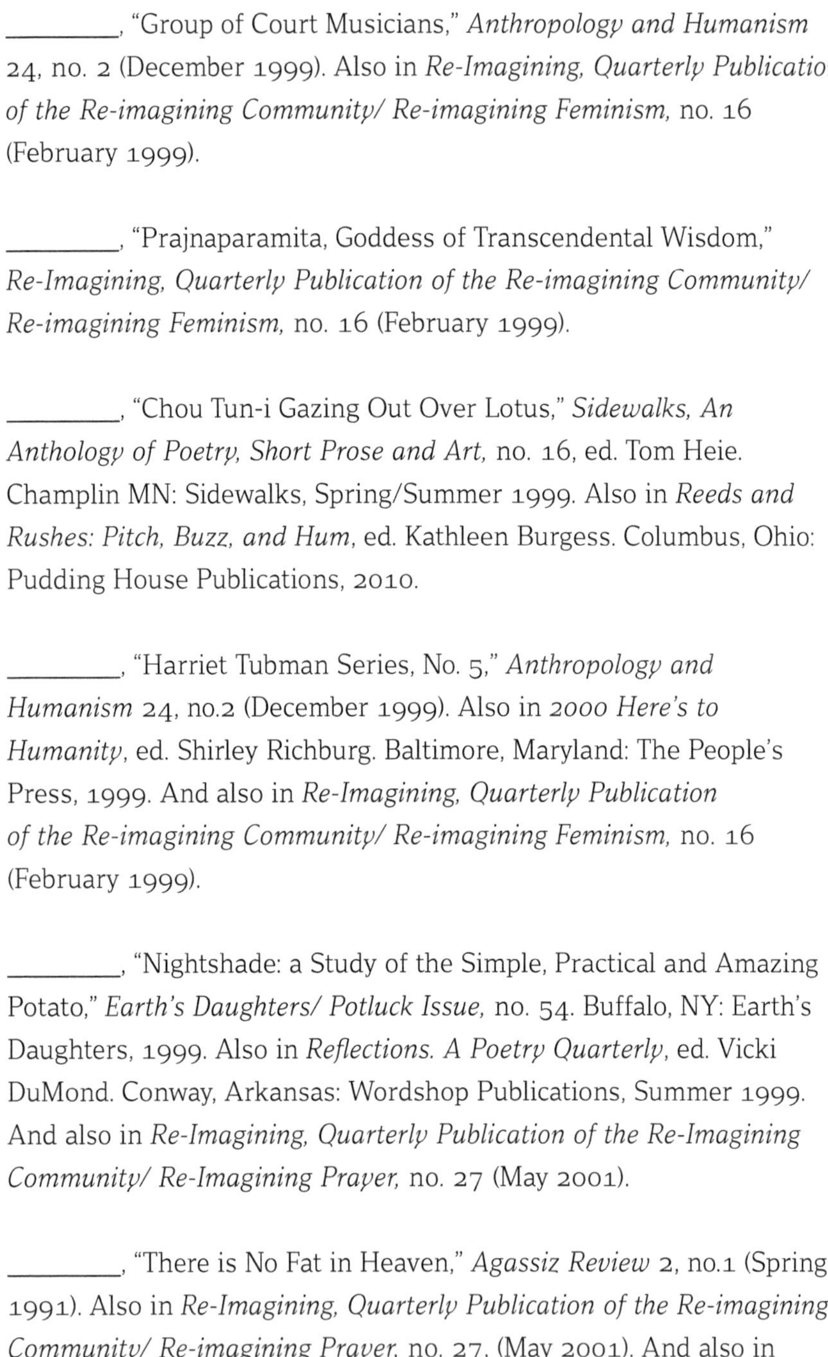

________, "Group of Court Musicians," *Anthropology and Humanism* 24, no. 2 (December 1999). Also in *Re-Imagining, Quarterly Publication of the Re-imagining Community/ Re-imagining Feminism,* no. 16 (February 1999).

________, "Prajnaparamita, Goddess of Transcendental Wisdom," *Re-Imagining, Quarterly Publication of the Re-imagining Community/ Re-imagining Feminism,* no. 16 (February 1999).

________, "Chou Tun-i Gazing Out Over Lotus," *Sidewalks, An Anthology of Poetry, Short Prose and Art,* no. 16, ed. Tom Heie. Champlin MN: Sidewalks, Spring/Summer 1999. Also in *Reeds and Rushes: Pitch, Buzz, and Hum,* ed. Kathleen Burgess. Columbus, Ohio: Pudding House Publications, 2010.

________, "Harriet Tubman Series, No. 5," *Anthropology and Humanism* 24, no.2 (December 1999). Also in *2000 Here's to Humanity*, ed. Shirley Richburg. Baltimore, Maryland: The People's Press, 1999. And also in *Re-Imagining, Quarterly Publication of the Re-imagining Community/ Re-imagining Feminism,* no. 16 (February 1999).

________, "Nightshade: a Study of the Simple, Practical and Amazing Potato," *Earth's Daughters/ Potluck Issue,* no. 54. Buffalo, NY: Earth's Daughters, 1999. Also in *Reflections. A Poetry Quarterly*, ed. Vicki DuMond. Conway, Arkansas: Wordshop Publications, Summer 1999. And also in *Re-Imagining, Quarterly Publication of the Re-Imagining Community/ Re-Imagining Prayer,* no. 27 (May 2001).

________, "There is No Fat in Heaven," *Agassiz Review* 2, no.1 (Spring 1991). Also in *Re-Imagining, Quarterly Publication of the Re-imagining Community/ Re-imagining Prayer,* no. 27, (May 2001). And also in

Gastronomica. The Journal of Food and Culture 3, no. 4. Berkeley: The University of California Press, Fall 2003.

________, "Vanitas: Flesh Dress for an Albino Anorectic," *The Lone Wolf Review* 3, no.1 (1999). Also in *Earth's Daughters/ Potluck Issue,* no. 54. Buffalo, NY: Earth's Daughters, 1999. And also in *Mined* 2, no. 1 (2001).

________, "Without Words," *Reflections. A Poetry Quarterly*, ed. Vicki DuMond. Conway, Arkansas: Wordshop Publications, Summer 1999. Also in *Mined* 2, no. 1 (2001).

________, "She Was Tired of Filling Her Heart with Hopeless Dreams," *Re-imagining, Quarterly Publication of the Re-imagining Community/ Re-imagining Feminism,* no. 16 (February 1999).

________,"Vanilla Geyser," *Mined* 2, no.1 (2001).

________, "Looking Glass Pictures," *Mined* 2, no. 1 (2001).

________, "Guardian Angels: Some Invented Families in Late 20th Century North America," *Mined* 2, no.1 (2001).

________, "My Infant Grandson," *Mined* 2, no.1, (2001).

________, "Mother and Child," *Re-imagining, Quarterly Publication of the Re-imagining Community/ Re-imagining Feminism,* no. 16 (February 1999).

________, "She Arrived Like a Long-Lost Cousin," *Crucible* 32. Wilson, NC: Barton College, Fall 1996. Also in *Me and My Angel,* ed. P. J. Roberts. Rockport, MA: Sandstar, 1996.

________, "Dream Fragments," *Mined* 2, no. 1 (2001).

________, "An Angel Before," *Me and My Angel*, ed. P. J. Roberts. Rockport, MA: Sandstar, 1996.

________, " Ode to Three Pillows," *Anthropology and Humanism Quarterly* 15, no. 4 (December 1990).

________, "Lessons in Bipedalism," *Anthropology and Humanism Quarterly* 16, no. 4 (December 1991).

________, "Boys Prepare for Life," *Poetry Motel Wallpaper,* no. 38 (1993).

________, " Hiking in the Shenandoah," *The Wolf Head Quarterly* 3, no. 4 (Autumn 1997).

________, " An Occasional Cup of Coffee," *The Sunday Suitor Poetry Review,* no. 6 (October 1997). Also in *Coffee and Chicory*, no. 7 (Fall/Winter 1997).

________, "On a Night," *The Southwest Journal* (July 1993).

________, " Thinking Twice," *Wisconsin Dialogue, A Faculty Journal for the University of Wisconsin-Eau Claire* 10 (1990).

________, " For the Dancer Mikhail Baryshnikov in Kafka's 'Metamorphosis,'" *Wisconsin Dialogue, A Faculty Journal for the University of Wisconsin-Eau Claire* 10 (1990).

________, " Hiroshima Remembrance," *The Southwest Journal* (July 1993).

________, " approaching hospice," *Frogpond, the Journal of the Haiku Society of America* 37, no.2 (Spring/Summer 2014).

________, "counting open lids," *Take-out Window. Haiku Society of America 2014 Members' Anthology*, ed. Gary Hotham. New York: Haiku Society of America, 2014.

________, "unable to climb," *Frogpond, the Journal of the Haiku Society of America* 36, no. 3 (Autumn 2013).

________, "Ayurvedic spa," *Frogpond, the Journal of the Haiku Society of America* 37, no. 1 (Winter 2014).

The collage on the front cover combines images from "Poet with Birds" by Marc Chagall, "Prajnaparamita, Goddess of Transcendental Wisdom" and "Female Shaman," all of which are in the permanent collection of the Minneapolis Institute of Arts, Minneapolis, Minnesota.

About the Author

Caroline Giles Banks, born in Boston, Massachusetts, was educated at Wellesley College, the University of New Mexico, the University of Minnesota, and the University of Chicago. Dr. Banks is a cultural anthropologist by training and profession and was on the faculties of the University of Wisconsin-River Falls and Luther College in Decorah, Iowa. Her poetry is often informed by her anthropological research and training. She is the author of *Warm Under the Cat: Haiku and Senryu Poems*; *The Clock Chimes: Haiku and Senryu Poems*; *The Weight of Whiteness: A Memoir in Poetry*; *The Clay Jar: Haiku, Senryu and Haibun Poems*; and *Tigers, Temples and Marigolds: Haiku and Haibun Poems*. Her award-winning poems have been published in numerous anthologies, literary magazines and journals. She lives in Minneapolis, Minnesota.

www.ingramcontent.com/pod-product-compliance
Lightning Source LLC
LaVergne TN
LVHW050538100826
845148LV00002B/606

* 9 7 8 0 9 6 4 5 2 5 4 7 4 *